House Beautiful

FIREPLACES

THE EDITORS OF HOUSE BEAUTIFUL MAGAZINE

LOUIS OLIVER GROPP
Editor in Chief

MARGARET KENNEDY
Editor

Text by
CAROL COOPER GAREY

HEARST BOOKS ■ NEW YORK

It is the policy of William Morrow and Company,
Inc., and its imprints and affiliates, recognizing the
importance of preserving what has been written, to
print the books we publish on acid-free paper, and
we exert our best efforts to that end.

Library of Congress Cataloging-in-Publication Data

Garey, Carol Cooper.
     House Beautiful Fireplaces / editors of House
Beautiful ; Carol Garey.
          p. cm.

     ISBN 0-688-16950-3
     1. Fireplaces. 2. Interior decoration.
I. House Beautiful.
     II. Title.   III. Title: Fireplaces.
     NA3050.G27   1999
     721'.8—dc21   99-23317
                                         CIP

Printed in the United Kingdom

FIRST EDITION

1   2   3   4   5   6   7   8   9   10

Edited by Alanna Stang
Designed by Susi Oberhelman

Produced by Smallwood & Stewart, Inc., New York, NY

www.williammorrow.com
www.housebeautiful.com

FIREPLACES ARE KEYNOTES OF CREATIVITY

IN THE HISTORY OF DECORATION.

LIKE NOTHING ELSE IN A HOUSE, THEY WRAP

UP A WIDE VARIETY OF DECORATIVE

AND ARCHITECTURAL NEEDS AND DESIRES.

GIVEN THIS ENORMOUS SIGNIFICANCE,

THEY DESERVE SERIOUS ATTENTION.

—MARK HAMPTON

CONTENTS

FOREWORD

WHO AMONG US doesn't love to sit by the fire, bewitched by the graceful, breathtaking dance of its flames, warmed by its elemental magic? It's a place I go to often: sometimes for stimulating conversation with friends; sometimes alone with a really good book; sometimes with just one special person—my wife, a daughter—for an important talk, where intimacy is invited.

But even when there is no fire, the fireplace remains a commanding presence, the natural focal point of almost any room. Furnishings must be arranged around it, its mantelpiece and surrounds designed with care, its decorative and emotional importance never underestimated, for sooner or later, everyone's attention will fasten there.

And so *House Beautiful Fireplaces* takes a loving look at this special spot in our homes. With provocative quotes from knowing people in the world of design—from architect Frank Lloyd Wright to decorator Mark Hampton—Carol Cooper Garey's text guides us through hundreds of handsome photographs, each chosen to illustrate the diversity and beauty of the fireplace. It is our hope that the ideas culled from the best work of the design professionals featured will stir memories of special times around the hearth, enrich its magical powers to enchant and soothe, and encourage new and unique interpretations of its design potential.

LOUIS OLIVER GROPP
Editor in Chief

House Beautiful

FIREPLACES

STYLE

FROM ITS MANTEL

to the glow of its flames,

the fireplace ignites

the mood of a room. It is

the opening statement,

the center of energy.

Working or not, it always

has a presence, and

its style often dictates the

tenor of the entire

room, whether through

grandiose or simple design.

Designer Celeste Cooper chose
pale maple to frame a minimalist
fireplace and imbue the room
with quiet elegance, above.

Architect Bruce Bernbaum
and designer Emily Summers infused
a contemporary house with Deco-
style refinement by adding step-
down limestone molding to a basic
fireplace, opposite.

Previous page, New York
designer Thomas O'Brien found his
home in a prewar apartment
with soaring windows and eighteen-
foot ceilings. He reinvented the
fireplace in deep brown marble
and oak to simultaneously project
age and modernity.

H A R M O N Y H A S B E E N the desired effect of
interior design since the 1600s, when the arrangement
of a room became a conscious effort to please the senses.
The ubiquitous fireplace, so utilitarian at first, eventually
became a mark of status, and a pivotal feature from which
the decorating plan evolved: Where to place a sofa or perhaps a chaise and coffee table? How to angle the furniture
to establish comfortable groupings? What objects set on
and around the mantel would best enhance the room?

What separates the predictable from the innovative is attention to scale, texture, and balance. Savvy
designers play on the theatrics of a fireplace, creating a
stage of the surrounding area. A sleek and streamlined
mantel might stand out next to a traditional dining room
table and chairs; a modernist's media room might house
audio and video entertainment in custom cabinetry on
either side of a comforting fire. Even the over-the-mantel
mirror, something of a decorating cliché, might get new
life as a mirrored surround instead.

There is no doubt the fireplace can prescribe a
room's character. The country hearth, an age-old symbol
of hospitality, evokes warmth with its seasoned timbers
and rustic texture. Enthusiasm for country houses is kin-
dled by such old-fashioned features as original mantels
and stone surrounds. Rooms of the less-is-more school
treat fireplaces as sculptural accessories to pared-down
furnishings. Strong, understated materials and clean-
lined contours are the hallmarks of the minimalistic

approach; a simple raised hearth can serve as a seating ledge as well as a surface for displaying a few prized objects. To turn a fireplace into the meditative focus of a serene room, furniture might be limited to only one or two pieces. Style is, after all, an editing process and a balancing act. According to the tenets of decorating, harmony is as much a result of subtraction as it is of addition. Some fireplaces defy convention altogether, becoming art forms on the drawing boards or in the hands of innovative decorators.

The gallery-like fireplace wall in a new suburban house, opposite, was integrated into the room's grid by architects Gisue and Mojgan Hariri. Its stone hearth, raised to the level of a coffee table, serves as a naturally lit display area for selected objects.

Fashion designer Geoffrey Beene juxtaposed a bronze mantel with a bold triangular mirror, above, to achieve what he calls "soft geometry."

The owners of this 1820 stone farmhouse in Pennsylvania were determined to resurrect its original character. With designer Laura Bohn, they achieved a level of comfort appropriate to the antiquity of the house. An austere church settle and rustic living room fireplace both reflect the owners' desire for romanticized simplicity. In the dining room, above, a hutch table with country Windsor chairs feels right at home in front of the rudimentary fireplace surrounded with rough-hewn barn timbers. The timbered mantelpiece is topped with Tennessee pottery and a nineteenth-century photograph of the original farm.

When white paint is applied to old brick fireplaces, years can be subtracted from their age and new style added to the rooms they inhabit. It certainly gave one little place in Sonoma, California, above, an air of city sophistication: "Urbane in the middle of nowhere," says its designer and owner, Orlando Diaz-Azcuy. He completed the city mood with muted tones and the moderated symmetry of two Piranesi prints, matching terra-cotta pots, and twin slipcovered armchairs. ▪ Five coats of white paint later, designer Spruce Roden managed to erase the gloom from his Connecticut fireplace, opposite. By adding a white frieze of acorns and oak leaves to a newly plastered ceiling and furnishing the space with a selection of comfortably stuffed and brightly upholstered armchairs, he endowed the room with a fresh take on the traditional.

With its yawning fireplace, a welcoming room designed by DD Allen, left, exudes warmth, inviting visitors to curl up in a chair and relax. Clearly, it is a place for reading by the fire. The elegantly carved mantelpiece is a work of art in itself and doesn't need much elaboration. A simple oval mirror and quaint accessories encourage the roaring fire to dominate the scene.　"Fresh milk" paint emphasizes the classical pillars and molding of a Federal-style fireplace, above, whose mantel serves as a small gallery for decorative objects. Original windowed cabinets frame the fireplace and provide handsome storage for collector Michael Berkowitz's treasures, which include elk's antlers and a tramp art mirror frame.

Large plain fireplaces run the risk of looking like black holes. In a New York City apartment, the design firm Bilhuber, Inc., avoided that trap by mirroring the major walls, thus seemingly doubling the room's size and balancing the flameless fireplace's impact. Above the well-proportioned surround, which is covered with wood-pulp paper, a sculpture of wooden forms once used for the casting of metal gears moves the energy of the fireplace upward and adds to the room's harmonious eclecticism. The graphic cream, black, and dark-chocolate color scheme plays off the bold design of the fireplace wall.

Two matching stone fireplaces at opposite ends of a grand New York City drawing room could have easily encouraged a formal symmetry, but designer Mariette Himes Gomez, master of the elegantly idiosyncratic, deftly resisted the obvious. Instead of setting them up as identical bookends, she treated them as if they were fraternal twins. One has mirrors flanking a framed drawing and an upholstered coffee table, left, while the other is set off by a large mirror, drawings grouped on one side, and a small coffee table, above. After hanging matching French, gilded lanterns from the ceiling on either end of the room, she created separate but equal seating arrangements, giving the fireplaces individual identities within a well-balanced context.

Nothing is as authentically evocative of Southwestern style as the fireplaces of the early adobe dwellings. Michael Reynolds integrated the fireplace into a wall with shelves that wittily suggest a mantel, opposite, a trick that complements the earthy design. The fireplace recalls pioneer days, when it would have been the principal source of heat. This ecologically oriented New Mexican house, however, receives its electricity and hot water through active solar energy systems. In designer Melanie Martin's California house, above, the corner fireplace and chimney were newly created by architect Jerry Allen Kler for a master bedroom that pays homage to the traditional clay houses in a cultured manner. Stacks of logs fill the curved hearth with rough-hewn textures that naturally suit the room.

In the refreshingly spare sun-streaked spaces of a St. Tropez retreat designed by architect Gae Aulenti, fireplaces are elevated to an art form. Framed and floating on the walls, the austere rectangles function as the rooms' focal points. In the dining room, above, Aulenti enclosed the firebox with sand-colored stucco and blond stone. The owner then enlivened the space with deep-red, straight-back antique chairs and a classic Eero Saarinen table. In the living room, opposite, Mediterranean blue doors and two intensely patterned sofas offset the serenity of a blank wall, an aesthetically appropriate background for the pale fireplace.

In a nonconformist 1950s ranch house creatively reinvented by San Francisco designer April Sheldon for a couple of risk-taking clients, two fireplaces reveal an imaginative spirit. In the living room the original board-and-batten fireplace, above, was updated with the addition of a colorful mosaic surround comprised of odd-shaped tile fragments. The second fireplace commands a prominent place in the family room, right, once the house's garage. In this multipurpose room, the unusual fireplace, constructed of split-face concrete, is kept company by a sandbag-turned-lampshade, a red entertainment cabinet on wheels, and a floor of three-foot plywood squares. The coffee table, another hybrid, is concrete infused with green rocks and brass screws that was formed into a slab and then polished to mimic fossilized stone.

"THE FIREPLACE

is the geometric and sym-

bolic center of the house,

for here is where the

sacred flame of the family

is kept burning," wrote

Thomas Beeby in *The Nature*

of Frank Lloyd Wright.

"It is the cosmic center

of the house where all

the forces of the landscape

are concentrated."

THE EMPHASIS ON THE integration of fireplaces in architecture dates back to the Renaissance. In the centuries since, architects have explored a huge range of design possibilities, from the rustic to the ultramodern. Today, these efforts have produced a new generation of fireplaces, in a wealth of materials. Stone and brick are still favored for their endurance and natural variations. Native stone, particularly if it's harvested from the ground on the building site, is often irresistible to architects. Indeed, there have been rocks unearthed that had "fireplace" written on them before a house was even built—"the fire burning deep in the masonry of the house itself," in Wright's words.

Charles Eames and Eero Saarinen's landmark 1949 Case Study House #9, left, is a classic of the modern movement. A glass-walled box overlooking the ocean in California, the house was carefully restored by architect Barry Berkus and is furnished with pieces arranged to give prominence to the all-important fireplace.

Previous page, architect Merrill Elam punctuated the serene screened-in porch of a modern Appalachian retreat with a thick concrete column that functions both as fireplace and indoor grill, and a split boulder that serves as a hearth.

Stone of a more refined nature suits minimalist architecture. Limestone, marble, slate, and granite are popular choices for sleek designs. Plaster is a versatile medium that mixes well with color and easily forms interesting textures. Metal, as applicable to fireplaces as it is to roofs, is often chosen for its reflective qualities, and can be used to create free-form sculpture. Charles Eames and Eero Saarinen paved the way for metal fireplaces with their case study houses and molded furniture of the 1940s.

In this era of experimentation and high technology, the fireplace—whether a period specimen or a modern abstraction—can be anything we want it to be.

To accommodate the client's request for a greenhouse-like space on their California oceanfront lot, architect Rob Wellington Quigley created a glass pavilion, opposite. The concrete fireplace wall anchors the sun-drenched spread and holds its own alongside a mobile by Alexander Calder.

Honoring the panorama of his Phoenix, Arizona, site, architect Jack DeBartolo designed a horizontal fireplace to be as mesmerizing as the view, above.

Some fireplaces owe their solid character to local stone and intrepid designers. In a great room styled on the ruggedly handsome Adirondack lodges, Jefferson B. Riley of Centerbrook Architects designed a local fieldstone wall as the indoor focus, opposite. Vertical slabs crown the fireplace, moving the visual energy toward the voluminous ceiling. ■ Inspired by Bernard Maybeck's 1921 High Sierras Lodge, architect John Grable of Lake/Flato produced the fireplace wall, above, using stones gathered on the property of the Texan ranch house it graces.

In a pocket of Northern California, where the orchards are organic, the air clean, and the bread home-baked, a fireplace in this rammed-earth house by David Easton lives up to the high standards of its naturalistic environment. Endowed with a narrowed tilted flue and splayed sides and back, right, it imparts heat in the cleanest and most efficient manner. The post-and-beam frame is concrete, as is the etched fireplace wall trimmed with gray-stained decay-resistant wood. Fireproof doors, above and below left, keep soot where it belongs and encase the fireplace when it is not in use.

In a house high above Los Angeles, architect J. Frank Fitzgibbons elevated the angular fireplaces to accentuate the dramatic vertical views from the three-story villa. They are accessories to the limitless vista, their basic geometric forms grounding the lofty space. In the master bedroom, opposite, the distant horizon is set off by the lines of the fireplace and its clean, geometric surround. In the living room, above, the fireplace zigzags on angles toward the window, punctuating the view.

Homes and fireplaces of a certain age can benefit from facelifts. Take the case of a Victorian house in Washington, D.C., above. Stripping the place of its old dark wood paneling and confining rooms, designer Gary Lovejoy created an airy duplex, highlighted by a crisp, contemporary fireplace. Chairs draped in striped sheets form a unit with the graphic black-and-white surround. ▪ A 1902 house in San Francisco is equipped for the future, now that its kitchen and family room have been fused, opposite. Designed by Daen Scheiber, the forty-foot space owes its feeling of intimacy to the fireplace. Surrounded by granite and framed in custom pewter molding, it has become part of the entertainment unit, which cleverly extends via the banquette to a cozy seating area.

An 1898 book on interior decoration noted that good taste in a house is revealed by the means used for heating it—namely the fireplace.

A modern arbiter of good taste, John Saladino takes the rustic fireplace to a high level of refinement, opposite. Surrounded by the distinctive texture of his signature scratchcoat plaster walls, and accentuated by hand-hewn Douglas fir beams and bluestone floors, the fireplace adds dimension to what is actually a multipurpose outdoor room. A corroded cast-iron seashell over the mantel is the designer's subtle reference to the room's part-time life as a pool house.

Early fireplaces were not only charged with heating but with cooking as well. One such heirloom from the 1700s, above right, incorporates a walk-in firebox, cupboards, and paneled folding doors. Designer Laura Bohn added a rough-cut cedar table surrounded by mismatched chairs.

With its walnut folding doors shut, below right, Monique and Sergio Savarese's 1840s fireplace provides a humble background for their kinetic furniture: a dining table with African-inspired legs and a coconut chair from Bali.

A whimsical neo-Palladian guesthouse, left, built by antique collector Gep Durenberger on a lot adjacent to his former Southern California home, exudes grace and stature thanks to the Louis XVI mantelpiece he installed in the structure he refers to as a "Gothick folly."   The living room of an eighteenth-century farmhouse in Provence is animated by its stucco fireplace, above. Paris decorator Jacques Grange designed the rough-hewn surround specially for the rustic space, which was once a shed for livestock. Aged beams and terra-cotta floors helped Grange preserve the original character of the space. To complete the scene, he introduced a playful bull—an allusion to the room's former function as well as an homage to Picasso, who lived in the region.

Custom-pigmented stucco forms a rectangular fireplace in a two-story beachfront living room, opposite. Designed by architect Steven Ehrlich, the chimney extends skyward via shoji-like insulated fiberglass panels. The fireplace is in harmony with the lightness of its surroundings, reflecting the tones and textures of the seascape facing this Southern California home.

Stones once used for boundary fences on rocky New England farms transform a Massachusetts living room fireplace into a monumental tribute to nature, above. The massive chimney rises like a steeple, reinforcing the scale of the double-height room designed by Debora K. Reiser.

IT HAS BEEN SAID THAT houses should have prominent chimneys and fireplaces, and the larger the house, the larger the chimney. The chimney declares its importance and demands the respect it has earned since man first devised a means to have fire indoors and smoke outside.

The smoky chimneys of nineteenth-century houses were cause for irritation—and invention. A titled American named Count Rumford concluded that the

proportions of domestic fireplaces were all wrong—specifically, the flue was too wide relative to the fireplace opening, and most heat was lost from the fire burning too high up the chimney. His solution: a narrowed flue with a base no more than four inches deep and a mantel opening about fourteen to twenty inches above the flames. "Reduce the fireplace and the throat of the chimney, or that part of which lies immediately above the fireplace, to a proper form and just dimensions," he proposed in his 1799 essay, "Upon Fireplaces." Over the centuries, the Rumford fireplace has often set the quality standard for architects and builders.

By abstracting the characteristics of Greek Revival, architect Hugh Newell Jacobsen created a new context for the chimney. The small houselike structure, opposite and right, refers to the *cella*, or internal sanctuary, of classical Greek temples. While in the ancient world the *cella* would have contained the statue of a deity, the chamber in this Ohio River house forms an enclosure for closets and bookshelves as well as a compact powder room.

With a freestanding fireplace, the chimney becomes a sculptural link between rooms. The loft-like rectangular room, opposite, designed by Texas architect Max Levy, depends on the geometric composition of the chimney and fireplace to establish boundaries between living and dining while unifying the space at the same time. Sculpture created by the owner is exhibited on the chimney wall. ▨ In a light-filled Northern California house, above, designed by Steven and Cathi House of the San Francisco architecture firm House + House, the fireplace is strategically placed between the living room on one level and the dining room a few steps up on another. Double-sided, the concrete and metal structure serves both areas with equal effect.

Three freestanding fireplaces soar to ceiling height thanks to the architectural integration of their chimneys. Each room is defined by the spaces carved around the internal chimney structures.

The San Francisco loft of designer Jonathan Straley, opposite, owes its well-defined dimensions to the chimney, which functions both as an art gallery and as a media storage unit (the television hides behind a hinged painting). The other side of the column has built-in bookshelves.

Two chimneys in a Chesapeake Bay house, designed by the Washington architect Stephen Muse, stand independently, allowing space to flow around them. In the bedroom, above right, the bed faces the fireplace and also looks out onto the porch behind. In the sitting room, below right, the chimney visually sets apart the windowed dining room beyond.

Water is the worthy attraction outside a Florida home designed by Jan Abell and Kenneth Garcia. The granite fireplace surround, situated under the large picture windows, draws attention to the outdoors; the external chimney stands away from the house, where it doesn't get in the way of the view. ▪ A mighty vista, opposite, is the bonus of this post-and-beam house designed by architects Jeffrey Biben and Peggy Bosley. Sited for optimum views of Oregon's Willamette River and unimpeded by the cylindrical chimney, the stone fireplace incorporates a Douglas fir hearth for seating and storage.

MANTELS

Designer Thomas O'Brien found a Greek Revival mantel, opposite, in an antiques store. Painted white to blend in with a whitewashed brick surround and underscored with a flagstone hearth, it fits right in with the living room fireplace in his 1928 Colonial cottage. An American beehive clock and French tole sconces from the 1820s top it off beautifully.

An American folk art mantel, above right, was a perfect fit for antiques dealer Toby West, a collector of nineteenth-century Americana and nautical artifacts. The turnings and carvings in the walnut suit the rich diversity of his collection.

HISTORY DOCUMENTS THE taste for huge mantels in the Renaissance, graceful ones in the eighteenth century, functional handcrafted ones in the nineteenth, and rescued ones in the twentieth. For those bent on period authenticity, or at least a trace of antiquity, the mantel is an ideal acquisition. It can provide a visual link between architecture and furnishings, and give a room a new proportion. It's also a wonderful place to showcase treasured family photographs, still life assemblages, or a changing collection of objets d'art.

Tile can work alchemy on a fireplace, as designer David Salomon demonstrated in his Long Island country house, opposite. The spicy blend of colors transforms the surround into a perfect complement to the rest of the room, an exotic tapestry of vibrant hues, diverse textures, and ethnic treasures from Mexican metal sconces to a tramp art mirror and a painted Indian screen.   The tiled fireplace in designer Sheila Bridges's 1901 apartment in a New York landmarked building, above, is a prized feature, its stately mantel and related paneling establishing the room's architectural heritage. The twin-column motif running down either side of the mantelpiece is echoed by a pair of tall, elegant columnar sculptures. Two prized Victorian side chairs complete the tableau.

A 1920s Spanish Colonial Revival style house in Los Angeles, renovated by architects Susan Lanier and Paul Lubowicki, wears its age on its original plaster mantelpiece, above. The carefully placed hand-painted vintage tiles are regally crowned with a carved mantel whose wood matches the vaulted beams.   An artistic variation on the tiled fireplace appears in a Cape Cod beach house designed by William Hodgins, right. The owners chose and sorted the handmade Portuguese tiles, which were then imbedded in the concrete surround. The bright colors and bold patterns studding the crisp white plaster make the fireplace playful and lively.

The innovative fireplace, whether playful, artistic, or dramatic, is a declaration of independent thinking. In designer Mariette Himes Gomez's Long Island barn house, opposite, a shelf pediment forms the mantel. A cast-iron bird sculpture by Illana Goor appears to float above the anvil-shaped surround. Anglo-Indian mahogany armchairs and a twig rocker offer unique fireside comforts in the country style of the minimalist for whom "chairs are like people." ▨ Industrial steel frames a fireplace conceived by designers Troy Walker and Jonathan Straley, above. Like the tubular aluminum frame bed positioned across from it, the striking metallic mantel expresses a highly modern sensibility, clear down to the hearth.

Though Stephen Shubel knows that "even the most talented designer cannot create natural light," his former 1,200 square-foot Berkeley, California, home is a testament to his willingness to try. By covering the fireplace surround with a wide swath of mirror, he managed to amplify the reflected light from the small-paned windows opposite it. The broad band of silvery glass also acts as a glamorous frame for what would otherwise be a less dynamic mantel. Blond wood floors, pale yellow slipcovers, a white coffee table, and an abundance of fresh-cut flowers augment the generous sunshine.

A tin pediment that once topped a New York City building was given new purpose in a California beach house by designers Joseph Lembo and Laura Bohn, opposite. Counterbalanced by an expansive wall and sky-high windows, the weathered mantel becomes sculpture in a room that puts this found object in a new, eye-level perspective. ▨ Another architectural element, a steel I-beam, satisfies the need for a mantel in a California hilltop house renovated by architect Dan Phipps, above. Phipps covered the brick fireplace with pigmented plaster and clad the hearth in steel plating. The setting evokes contemporary temples in Japan, where the owners once lived.

Rooms that inherit old mantels are richer for them. The turnings on this mantel, above, signs of early American craftsmanship, are particularly outstanding against an old brick wall painted white. Tall candlesticks balance the vertical composition. ■ A turn-of-the-century treasure, right, holds its own with early Gustav Stickley oak pieces and a rare 1905 corner cupboard. The brick surround, painted white, enhances the mellowed wood and a collection of antique ceramics.

The Arts and Crafts movement brought with it a passion for high-quality handmade features. A new generation of architects continues to draw inspiration from it today. New York architect Stephen Byrns, for example, infused a new house on the shore of Lake Michigan with heritage details. The wood and stone mantelpiece in the library, opposite above and below, with flattened, vertical moldings, bird's-eye maple decorative panels, and inlaid stones, is reminiscent of the Prairie houses of Frank Lloyd Wright. A sign of a house with soul, the mosaic was made of beach stones collected by the family. A bluestone fireplace in the living room, above and below right, also exhibits elements of the Prairie style in the artful detail of the stone niche.

HEARTH

A "rubble hearth" and its chimney salvaged from a deserted Maine house, opposite, is counterbalanced by an old watchmaker's sign hung high above the cross beam. Designers Mallory Marshall and James Light created a snug haven for humans in this space that was once the domain of peacocks.

Architect Peter Forbes's modern interpretation of the hearth uses blocks of stone to pave the bedroom floor of a Maine retreat, above, providing plenty of horizontal space for a warming stretch or a fireside nap.

WHILE THE WORD HEARTH means "home" to most of us, in its literal sense it refers to the floor of the fireplace or the area in front of it, usually a slab of stone or other fireproof material that protects the floor from soot and flying sparks.

In its more extravagant incarnations, the hearth can take form in any number of materials, shapes, and sizes. Along with its practical aspects, it works in tandem with the aesthetic of the fireplace, whether it's flush with the floor, recessed, raised, cantilevered, or even invisible. It can provide additional seating in a room or storage for fireplace supplies.

Zinc-coated panels form a multidimensional fireplace, above, that gains extra volume from its raised hearth. Made of stone, the hearth is twelve inches deep, creating adequate space to sit or place objects. Architect Laurence Booth related the industrial-gray fireplace facade to the metal roof and the dark stone hearth to the scored concrete floor.   A poured concrete slab resting casually on boulders anchors a fireplace wall, opposite. The thick, shelflike hearth contributes a sense of space and visual texture to an otherwise simple fireplace in the compact seating area of a San Francisco home designed by Lisa Weiss.

This raised hearth integrates
all of the elements of adobe-style
fireplaces in a Santa Fe home.
Designer Joe D'Urso uses the hearth
as an architectural bonus, a natural
extension of the floor and wall. A
stacking place for logs and a ledge
for a single sculptural tool, it
provides a step up to the fire—and
also to the television and stereo
equipment, cleverly screened by a
bleached-ash grid-form shutter. The
strong horizontal swath of hearth
balances the vertical shapes above
it. Sea grass matting defines the
conversation area in front.

Versatility and intimacy are built into a concrete hearth by architects Fernau and Hartman of Berkeley, California. Set just below the Douglas fir banquettes, it becomes an extension of the congenial seating arrangement. The lowered ceiling creates an intimate setting by the fire, a contrast to the banquette area where expansive windows open the space to the outdoors.

UTILITY

KEEPING THE HOME

fires burning demands

attention, maintenance,

and equipment. How we

care for the fireplace

is evident not only in its

visual impact but in

its performance. The utili-

tarian aspects of fireplace

stewardship are basic,

but the ancillary details can

turn an acceptable fireplace

into an outstanding one.

A nautical theme unifies the many fireplaces in a century-old Shingle Style beach house renovated by architect Samuel White and decorated by Jed Johnson and Alan Wanzenburg. In the living room, previous page, square sea-green tile sets off a shiny brass fender and bellows. The dining room fireplace is animated by playful mermaids and anchor-shaped andirons, above. In one bedroom, opposite, black andirons rise out from the fire hole.

CONSIDERING THAT NINETY percent of the heat generated by an average fireplace escapes out the chimney, there is good reason to focus on efficiency. One effective approach is to burn roaring fires rather than the low, smoldering variety. Hot fires heat the surrounding bricks; consequently, more heat reflects into the immediate area. How to make a fire with gusto? Begin with a layer of crumpled newspaper, then crisscross kindling on top. For the fire to receive oxygen, the newspaper and kindling need to be loose enough for air to circulate. Lastly, add three logs on top. Open the damper completely, make a torch of rolled newspaper, and wave the burning torch under the damper to heat the chimney air. The lighted torch can then be used to ignite the bed of newspaper.

A periodic inspection and cleaning of the fireplace is a necessary part of maintenance, as is the installation of a chimney cap to prevent animals from nesting in the flue. Once the infrastructure is tended to, tools and storage come into the picture. Andirons serve to hold wood in place and add visual interest to the fireplace setting. Screens are safety nets for falling logs; they too can dramatically enhance the fireplace's appearance.

Where to store the wood poses a challenge that can produce creative solutions, including hearths as platforms for handsome logs, antique buckets and baskets recruited for fireside service, or adjacent built-in bins—perhaps accessible from the outdoors.

THE SPRING IS NOT SO BEAUTIFUL THERE
BUT DREAM SHIPS SAIL AWAY
TO WHERE THE SPRING IS WONDROUS RARE
AND LIFE IS GAY

THE SPRING IS NOT SO BEAUTIFUL THERE
BUT LADS PUT OUT TO SEA
WHO CARRY BEAUTIES IN THEIR HEARTS
AND DREAMS, LIKE ME

A classical fireplace in a new home by Robert Hammond is articulated by an antique standing screen, opposite. Iron scrollwork, reminiscent of gates on country estates, is a dramatic presence in the room whether the fire is blazing or not.

In the manner of an English country house, a fireplace has a fire basket and fender among its refinements, above. Bellows are stationed nearby to boost the fire, above which hydrangeas hang to dry.

THE TOOLS THAT STOKE, protect, and groom make a fireplace's operation more efficient—and often more stylish. To paraphrase Edith Wharton, the effect of a fireplace depends on the appropriateness of its accessories. She declared that andirons should harmonize with the design of the mantel and be in scale with its dimensions.

Serious or fanciful, ornate or plain, fireplace tools have earned their keep ever since the thirteenth century when fire screens were used as heat shields. Fire baskets, fenders, screens, and utensils dress the fireplace in everything from iron to highly polished brass. Andirons, or firedogs, once essential to the support of spits for cooking, have become highly collectible objects of ornamentation.

Painter Chuck Fischer sparks the fire of his New York apartment, above left, with rounded brass andirons that resemble old radio microphones. Their stout modern shape keeps logs secure and relates to the shimmering silver globes perched atop the mantel.

"Any element is more exciting when you juxtapose it with something that doesn't seem logical," says Mariette Himes Gomez. She demonstrates the validity of her assertion with an oversize pair of bulbous coal black andirons that play up a demure undersize fireplace, below left.

A Louis XVI lime-stone mantel and nineteenth-century French andirons transform an ordinary living room into a spectacular example of the power of innovative design thinking, opposite. The original forged iron crossbar is decorative and practical: It can be removed to stoke the fire.

Worldly goods embellish the fireplace, opposite, in a New York City apartment designed by Robert Couturier. The owners' penchant for shells is revealed in silvered andirons and golden Venetian grotto chairs. Brass tools contribute to the richness of the plaster and marble fireplace, which is crowned by an eighteenth-century mirror.   Aglow in a yellow bedroom, the neoclassical fireplace, designed by John Wilson for an upstate New York house, is equipped with a sunny disposition, above. A handsome set of brass fireplace utensils looks smart against the black granite surround, and a pair of unusual canine andirons stand as guardians of the fire.

"I like lots of air, order, personal objects, and beautiful architecture," says William Hodgins. He also clearly enjoys interesting fire baskets and other esoteric accoutrements, judging from the adornment of various fireplaces in his two Massachusetts abodes. An iron fire basket contains the fire's brilliance, above left, while silver andirons reflect the flames. A tall fire basket nearly reaches the height of the rising fire, below left. A brass fire basket and globe illuminate the dark surround of a seventeenth-century French stone mantel, right.

Modern-style fireplaces need little in the way of accessories; by design, they should be clutter-free. A classic folding screen serves the clean-lined fireplace handsomely, opposite; it protects the full expanse of the opening and adds a subtle gleam to the austere wall.   A good example of the less-is-more credo is the fireplace wall of masonite that David Anthony Easton designed and painted to resemble bronze, above. It's equipped with wall-mounted lamps that supplement the firelight. A simple standing screen adds dimension to the flush mantel and its stack of logs.

Whimsical screens that refuse to take themselves too seriously add a note of surprise and delight to their surroundings. No conventional screen would do for Tom Parr, former chairman of the legendary decorating firm of Colefax & Fowler, whose house in southern France is a relaxed version of an eighteenth-century pavilion built for Madame de Pompadour. His passion for fabrics carries through to the fireplace, opposite. Unabashedly decorative, the tromp l'oeil fabric and chinese vase screen stands in during the off-season and can be moved to accent another area when it's time to fire up.

Creative license is also the prerogative of former fashion designer Kristin Perers, who makes light of a conventional screen by folding paper into a pleated fan, or "fire paper," in her London home, right.

The Victorians didn't take kindly to empty hearths, thus the invention of the painted fire board, a decorative panel that also protects against soot and drafts.

In designer Alexandra Stoddard's home, fireplaces become frames for exuberant bouquets, reflecting her passion for flowers and beautiful details. Stoddard responds to her perennial question, "When is the last time your room laughed?" with a painted basket of geraniums spilling from a sitting room fireplace, above left, and a picturesque arrangement of wildflowers showering her country bedroom with cheer, below left. In a second sitting room, opposite, a fire board is ablaze with painted hydrangeas looking as robust as the fresh-picked bunch in a pitcher nearby.

An overabundance of trees on designer Stephen Mallory's property provided several seasons' worth of logs. When his stone cottage was renovated, he incorporated the wood in the most natural way possible: stacked alongside the fireplace where it belongs, opposite.

A ready supply of kindling is propped in a crock near a rustic fireplace, above, suiting the style that gives the Manhattan apartment the air of a country retreat.

"BEECHWOOD FIRES ARE bright and clear if the logs are kept a year; chestnut's only good, they say, if for long 'tis laid away." So goes an old rhyme. Ever since logs replaced coals, we've been devising shelters to preserve, protect, and store them. For the sake of neatness and containment, wood may have its own home recessed in a fireplace wall. When no built-in storage exists, other solutions can be devised: stacking on the hearth, piling in buckets, or standing in pails. Standard operating procedure calls for a variety of wood sizes, including kindling, and an ample supply of newspaper, all of which should have their own storage areas.

In a country house facing the Blue Ridge Mountains, logs are an integral part of the textural environment. Indeed, for designer Nancy Braithwaite, they go hand in hand with a rustic way of life and the daily workings of the living room fireplace. Here the log storage is a casual arrangement of freestanding shelves stacked with bins of kindling—a merging of old timber with the room's weathered post-and-beam construction. The mantel, left, discovered at an antiques market, wears green paint that complements the display of Audubon Catesby prints. Trays worn with age, above, hold a ready supply of kindling for the adjacent fire.

The best of both worlds: Marcel Breuer, whose visionary architecture was a collaboration with nature, created a built-in unit for storing wood as part of a concrete fireplace, opposite. Cast in place and then bush-hammered to reveal the individual pebbles and gravel, the fireplace is in the family room of a house designed by Breuer in 1959 and restored by Jonathan Foster.   A New Mexico house designed by Wayne Lloyd, with interiors by Joyce Crawford, presents a modern take on the indigenous beehive fireplace, above. Built-in shelves house stacked logs, which resonate with the rough-hewn columns and beams.

DESIGN

WHILE THE fireplace may be the central focus of a room, it won't make a truly effective design statement without the support of a host of other elements. Wall treatments and lighting, color schemes and textures, furniture style and placement— all must cooperate to give the fireplace its due.

As the traditional focus of comfort in the home, the fireplace is intrinsically full of appealing qualities. How those qualities translate into suitable, comfortable design is the point designer Billy Baldwin addressed when he said, "Comfort to me is a room that works for you and your guests. It's deep upholstered furniture. It's having a table handy to put down a drink or a book. It's also knowing that if someone pulls up a chair for a talk, the whole room doesn't fall apart."

Designer John Saladino breaks rooms down into distinct zones, with the fireplace as one focus for seating. This principle is his way of humanizing the scale of very large rooms. Soft neutrals—or "nuance" colors as he calls them—contribute to the intimate environments that characterize his inglenooks, where richly upholstered furniture is positioned to take full advantage of the fire and the way the sunlight hits.

For Richard Lowell Neas, the room with a fireplace was an opportunity to create an illusion of grandeur with decorative paint techniques. Imaginative and witty, his design style emphasized details not necessarily found in the architecture.

Regardless of its style, the fireplace is a veritable magnet for the reader, the romantic, the spinner of tales. Indeed, it can be a refuge from the world at large, its accoutrements the epitome of comfort and suitability.

Part barn, part castle, a Long Island living room, opposite, exemplifies John Saladino's pride of place. The room is an assemblage of diverse materials with weathered posts and beams framing the fireplace.

Tina Beebe and Buzz Yudell apply the principle of fireplace as comfort zone in a kitchen sitting area, above. Casual wicker nudges up to the hearth, where the atmosphere is "nouveau Tuscan" farmhouse, despite the Southern California address.

Previous page, the colonnade-style mantelpiece in a bedroom designed by Simone Feldman and Victoria Hagan is in stately contrast to the rattan couch, informal greenery, and airy window dressing. The serene lavender walls bring all the elements together.

Quirky pieces of American ephemera fit perfectly with a Shelter Island fireplace, above, as well as its locale, a seaside community on Long Island. Designed by Carolyn Guttilla for a couple of unabashed fish lovers, the living room's white wainscoting suits the dark mantelpiece swimmingly. ▓ Hugh Newell Jacobsen's egg-crate bookcases endow a Florida living room, opposite, with literary ambitions as well as a pleasing sense of geometric organization.

WALLS

The curves and carvings of a marble mantel pop out against brilliant wall colors and graphic art, opposite. To achieve the wall's texture and tone, designer Mary Douglas Drysdale used a decorative dragging technique that involves applying a green base coat followed by a layer of subtler green.

In a room designed by Mark Hampton, above, intensely dark brown walls emphasize the stately fireplace. The mantel appears in relief, its details silhouetted against the painted backdrop.

FOR ALMOST EVERY FIREPLACE, there is a fireplace wall deserving of attention. Each is dependent on the other for support and visual impact. The fireplace leans on the wall for its sense of place, and the wall relies on the fireplace for its stature. The most successful designs take into account the scale of the room, its architectural details, and the relationship of each to the fireplace. Decorations also affect the degree of importance accorded the fireplace.

Molding and paneling can make considerable contributions to the fireplace, wholly integrating it into the room. And for brave spirits, strongly patterned wallpaper will create a dramatic backdrop for mantel and hearth.

The legendary eighteenth-century English farmhouse, Charleston, bears the artistry of its former inhabitants Vanessa Bell and Duncan Grant, the Bloomsbury duo who crafted exuberant wall designs with elaborate motifs. The freehand painting over the sitting room mantel, opposite, is evidence of Grant's prodigious talent. Designer Ronald Grimaldi accented the tall, graceful presence of a period mantel, above left, with nineteenth-century French chinoiserie wallpaper. The bucolic scene, set off by breezy curtains, frames the fireplace and slender mirror. Dark walls sharply define the all-white accents in a library set for festivity around the fire, above right. The mantel, its accessories, and adjacent bookshelves are clearly defined by the application of a contrasting color. White molding reiterates the classical theme of the mantelpiece and amplifies its visual impact.

Against paneled walls, fireplaces take on a refined and all-important air. For Thomas Britt, the more ornate the better. He devised the wall details in a high-ceilinged room, above, to enhance the splendid fireplace. Indeed, the elegant plaster molding, rococo mirrors, and extravagantly colored chandelier are in concert with the jewel of a mantel. ■ A modern-day interpretation of the well-mannered salon, opposite, elaborates on moldings, carvings, and columns fashioned of richly grained wood. Beverly and Rebecca Ellsley designed the magnificent fireplace, with its crowned mirror (which hides a slim silouette television), inlaid landscape paintings, and marble surround, as part of a grand scheme in which all the intricate details have mellowed into an ageless blend.

There's nothing shy about these wall flowers; they invite attention and actually make compact, low-ceilinged rooms appear more spacious.

Michael Stanley's farmhouse dining room walls, above left, are buoyant with flowered fabric and bows and swags on the mantel. Stanley's response to Connecticut's gray seasons? Perennial cabbage roses in the living room, below left. He tea-dyed the fabric to tone it down slightly, then applied one hundred yards of it to the walls. A turn-of-the century mantel painted linen white benefits from the background, as does an Italian gilded mirror and burl-framed dog prints from Paris.

"Cheery and lived-in" is the way designer Jane Churchill describes the dining room of her 1840s house, opposite. The mood is communicated by the fabric wallcovering and reflected in the Swedish mirror over the mantel.

Mirrors seemingly melt away the fireplace wall of a deceptively large Manhattan studio, left. Why no mirror over the mantel? "The illusion is ruined if you see yourself," says designer Tom Scheerer, whose street find, a large stretched-fabric disk, proudly commands the space. ■ A pair of douka wood cabinets that Marie-Paule Pellé calls "classics out of the general memory" establish the fireplace wall, above, as a dominant feature in a room that blazes even without a fire.

In a new library designed by
Celeste Cooper, opposite, the
limestone fireplace, inspired by a
1920s Jean Cocteau design, is
illuminated by low-voltage spot-
lights mounted on the side of
the ceiling beams. "The concept,"
she says, "is to focus light on
what you want to highlight, not
to light the room uniformly."

For Paris designer Frédéric
Méchiche, dramatization is as
important as illumination; he
chose a pair of dazzling French
crystal sconces to make an antique
fireplace shine, above.

BEFORE THERE WERE ELECTRIC lights to illuminate our lives, fires often performed the task. They were sparked in the morning at breakfast and burned until bedtime, providing all the voltage—and warmth—necessary for a day's activity. With the advent of the oil lamp in 1749, the role of the fireplace as the major source of light was somewhat diminished.

The challenge for decorators today is to work with colors and materials, keeping electric light, firelight, and natural light in mind—"to have the right light properly distributed so that the rooms may be suffused with just the proper glow, but never a glare," declared Elsie de Wolfe in 1913. No simple matter, of course, but invaluable advice.

The contemporary fireplace in
a Dallas, Texas, living room
orchestrated by designer Emily
Summers and architect Bruce
Bernbaum is living proof that
an inanimate object can
produce high drama when
given the spotlight. The spare
chimneypiece, whose absence
of ornament is its strength,
is lit indirectly from square-
paned window walls. An early
twentieth-century Arts and
Crafts carpet basks in the fire's
glow. The generous arcs of
light from above are balanced
by table lamps that serve
the seating arrangements and
cast additional light on the
exotic dark wood tables.

FURNITURE

In a Long Island home designed by Greg Jordan, a red-hot chair and matching oversize ottoman snuggle up to the fire, opposite; their bright color forms a natural affinity with the flames.

The bold 1930s style mantelpiece designed by Mariette Himes Gomez sets the tone for a richly appointed room, above. In color and proportion, the sumptuous brown leather bench and black coffee table refer back to the striking mantelpiece.

KNOWING WHAT A room needs is both an intuitive process and an exercise in creativity. Gifted designers can take a familiar scenario, like the living room with requisite fireplace, and devise a new approach.

Just as location is the rule of thumb in real estate, the positioning of furniture is the first consideration for a smart space. In the living room, this can translate into a fireplace bench adjacent to a coffee table. In the bedroom the fireplace may offer an opportunity for strategically placed easy chairs or a single chaise longue. In the kitchen, a fireplace might look more attractive from the vantage point of a fireside breakfast nook. Furniture placement around the prime real estate of the fireplace results in a higher value for the room.

The ultimate in English country style is conveyed by the casual combination of fabric and pattern in a hunting lodge leased from the National Trust. Furnished by Nicholas Haslam, the lodge's tiny sitting room, above, plays up the grand fireplace. Abundant seating is provided by plump sofas, slipper chairs, and a bench needlepointed by Haslam. ▨ A stately bedroom, right, radiates gracious living with its nineteenth-century mantelpiece from a New Orleans plantation house. Designer Lynn von Kersting positioned facing sofas, covered in sun-bleached cotton ruffles, to set off the gracefulness of the fireplace and complete the picture of comfort and leisure.

The only thing better than sitting by the fire is reclining by the fire. A romantic canopied bed cozies up to a wide-mouthed fireplace, above left. The softly undulating mantel looks just right in a boudoir.

A four-poster bed becomes a frame for a fireplace, below left—all the better to gaze at glowing embers late into the night. The vaulted room also offers a quiet spot for lounging under the curtained window within close range of the fireplace.

A feeling of utter calm is this bedroom's strong suit, opposite. The fireplace's simple stone frame is complemented by the sculptural sycamore bed. Angled as it is, the bed commands an unobstructed view of the fireplace. A single tall candlestick accents the serene surround; a sun-inspired mirror hangs over the mantel.

In the manner of early modern German architect Peter Behrens, architect Stephen Harby created a fireplace nook for his Southern California library, opposite, by combining banquettes with tables and soft, overstuffed chairs. Square panels marked off by flat molding establish a theme for the built-in seating, the fireplace surround, and displays of Asian folk-art masks. ▓ The grandeur of the fireplace in an eighteenth-century Palladian folly, above, is enhanced by elegant appointments. The weekend retreat of designer Veere Grenney, it offers an array of splendid antique chairs as well as modern banquettes for fireside seating under the carved rococo brackets and Roman busts.

THE URGE TO ADORN

a mantel is an irresistible

opportunity to put

personal taste and favorite

possessions on display.

For some, a single paint-

ing is eloquence enough;

for others, only a galaxy

of objects will do. The

choices are limitless; all

that's required is imag-

ination and a willingness

to experiment.

Fashion designer Michael Leva describes his style as soothingly austere. In his New York home, above, a gilt-wreathed mirror and a pair of tall lavender tapers turn the mantel into a shrine of serenity.

In the dining room of a house he designed in France, opposite, Richard Lowell Neas's noble limestone chimneypiece showed off his collection of faience china.

Previous page, the fireplace as a stage: Lilliputian bent wire chairs are fancifully assembled on a weathered mantel, dwarfing an old-fashioned clock and a petite bunch of flowers.

THE DECORATION OF fireplaces has evolved through the centuries from elaborate Jacobean coats of arms and other displays of wealth and status, to the neoclassicism of the seventeenth century, to postmodernism's spare and lean design. Today, no one set of rules applies.

What becomes a fireplace most? A painting or graphic poster, perhaps. A collection of found objects, souvenirs, or antiques. For those with a penchant for seasonal change, the fireplace is an ideal location for a flat of paperwhites or a garland of evergreens. But mantels need not be laden with worldly goods to make a strong impression; the modern fireplace that deliberately shuns ornamentation exhibits serenity and sense of order.

DISPLAY

For Carolyn Quartermaine, it is "the ambiguity of hidden layers" that inspires her assemblages, one of which animates her own mantel, opposite. In her inimitably quirky style, she arranged five pinecones on one side of a composition that includes a framed collage. A chair upholstered in one of her signature fabrics participates in the tableau.

Succinct and to the point, a vase of flowers perches on a sliver of marble in the living room, above, that Gilles Depardon and his wife Kathryn Ogawa designed for their family's retreat in Sardinia.

THE MANTEL OFFERS endless possibilities to create one still life or another. The hearth presents a backdrop against which any number of artistic arrangements can be assembled. For the insatiable collector, the display may run from candlesticks to clocks to a gallery's worth of old photographs. Sentimental treasures and family heirlooms personalize a whole room.

In the English school of decorating, the mantel becomes a repository for a great diversity of porcelains, pictures, and all manner of accessories. For those whose taste runs to more edited displays, one singular sensation—say an important vase or a striking piece of art—can become a mantel's sole pride and joy.

In the living room of a turn-of-the-century country house by Mariette Himes Gomez, above left, David Hockney's *Celia in an Armchair* dominates. ▪ In an elegant room by Mary Douglas Drysdale, above right, brightly colored walls set off an abstract canvas over the uncluttered mantel. The quirky little stool pulled up to the fire is totally unexpected in this classic setting. ▪ In Gary Lovejoy's apartment the fireplace has been turned into an artistic feast for the eyes, opposite. A sleek, geometric pedestal and bust is the perfect accompaniment to the spare, elegant fireplace and sculptural mirror.

The brazen scale of a larger-than-life leaf over a fireplace, above left, breathes life into a spare setting.

In a Manhattan sitting room by designer Gail Green, the huge head of a tulip plays off the color and curve of a modernist mantel, below left. A vase of life-size white tulips on the table seems to pay homage to the photographic star.

Like the void in an unlit fireplace, the dark, abstract canvas, opposite, evokes mystery and shadow. A garland eased across the mantel, a pinecone resting below, three pears in a row, and a gentle bouquet add texture to the setting designed by Frank Babb Randolph.

The art of mantel display can be a fantastic adventure in eccentric experimentation. For New Orleans furniture and accessories designer Angèle Parlange, it was the majestic decrepitude of the cracked black marble mantelpiece, above, in a French Quarter pied-à-terre that inspired her idiosyncratic arrangement of ornate silver vessels bearing bamboo shoots and antique pocket portraits from the Paris flea-market. ▓ On the soapstone mantel in her Connecticut living room, right, Gretchen Mann had no qualms about mixing rust with gilt and fine antiques with cast-off junk, then remixing ad infinitum. Twelve-foot ceilings leave plenty of space for a vintage clock-shaped jeweler's sign to dwell comfortably between two shapely aging finials, which add texture to the perpetual work in progress.

Scale plus symmetry equals drama. Jacques Grange's inspired mantel arrangement in a Paris apartment, above left, is a display tour de force; the magnanimous use of a tall mirror reflects the ceiling's detail, turns the Romanesque bust into two, and transforms a pair of statuesque lamps into four floating globes. ▪ Another triumph for a tall mirror, this one is teamed with twin obelisks and topiary of the same height, above right. ▪ A 1793 Paris flat decorated by Christian Liaigre is the picture of contemporary chic. Two slender lamps of Liaigre's own design give the sensuous mantel the impact of sculpture, opposite. With three pieces of art arranged asymmetrically between them, the compositional balance shifts slightly until the eye focuses on a demure pair of goblets or the smart twin benches below.

Fiercely house-proud, the Victorians deemed the fireplace a prime location for the enlarging effect of mirrors. The tradition still holds today, especially for stalwart collectors eager to maximize their proud possessions.

For Mario Buatta, "the bedroom is where you keep the things dearest to you." He hung a gilded oval mirror over the graceful fireplace, above left, and adorned it with a ribbon and bow to reflect the romantic finery and precious keepsakes he assembled in a dreamy New York boudoir.

Designer Sue Burgess's Washington, D.C., living room, below left, reflects her discretion; the refined fireplace, replete with dramatic mirror and dual sculptures, exhibits a synthesis of chosen pieces.

A heavily framed circular mirror magnifies Americana in a classic New England house, opposite. For Peter Ermacora and Evan Hughes, designers with a passion for old books and American vernacular furniture, their mantel becomes a miniature library.

In lieu of a fire, a crate of blooming bulbs becomes the center of attention in a sitting room, opposite, arranged by Libby Cameron. A refreshing change from wintry logs, the paperwhites can be cultivated on a window ledge and moved to the hearth when they blossom.

In a refined room by José Solis Betancourt, above, summertime greenery animates the dark hole of a classic white fireplace and accentuates the gracefulness of its andirons.

THE SEASONS OFFER A natural bounty that, in the hands of an inspired arranger, can become captivating decoration. Just how to bring seasonal energy to the empty hearth? "In my own case, an open Japanese umbrella suffices," wrote J. E. Panton in 1888. "The temperature in England changes so quickly and so often that I scarcely can feel fires are an impossibility; but quite a pretty change in the room can be made by . . . removing fender . . . and filling up the grate with great ferns and flowering plants or cut flowers, frequently changed, for nothing save the ubiquitous aspidistra lives comfortably in this lowly and draughty situation." Drafts aside, frequency of change ensures seasonal variety.

As soon as the season shifts away from snowy dampness and the fireplace is no longer actively engaged in a flaming dance, a classical mantelpiece can host an off-season spectacle of blooms. A blithe, bright bedroom designed by Charles Spada and Tom Vanderbeck recalls European resorts where fresh flowers would be delivered daily along with the bed linens. The blossoming hearth and cheerful bouquets of lilies of the valley are reminders of the early days of spring when white buds open and the trees get their first spray of green.

"IF THE EFFECT BE SATISFACTORY
TO THE EVE, THE SUBSTANCE USED
IS A MATTER OF INDIFFERENCE..."

EDITH WHARTON
JOHN CODMAN
THE DECORATION OF HOUSES

Floral designer Spruce Roden fires up the Halloween spirit around his rough-hewn fireplace and chimney wall, opposite, with giant pumpkins and an architectural garland of gathered pinecones. The exposed granite fireplace, circa 1788, seems right in tune with its seasonal decoration, a subtle flourish that appears to have happened quite naturally. ▪ Victoria Hagan's office mantel, above, celebrates the season that makes sugarplum fairies dance. Indeed, with her spirited designer magic, she transforms traditional Christmas greens and fruits into a festive winter display. Juniper leaves, limes, lemons, berries, and pears are heaped on a wooden mantel painted to look like stone. A French Empire clock and eighteenth-century brass candlesticks add authentic age to a mirror that, in a gesture apropos to the season, reflects a rising star.

Hung with stockings, strewn with yuletide goodies, or festooned with ripe fruit, fireplaces set the stage for a joyous holiday. In the living room of his former home, designer Richard Lowell Neas, who believed that "more is more," surrounded a roaring fireplace with a bounty of unclipped and unadorned evergreens. ▪ Artist-author Abbie Zabar arranged plump pears across a clean white mantel in her spare New York City apartment, above. Next to a Christmas tree decorated with handmade and heirloom ornaments, the fireplace needs nothing more than the humble fruit to celebrate the season of giving.

DIRECTORY OF DESIGNERS AND ARCHITECTS

Jan Abell
Abell-Garcia Architects
Tampa, Fla.
(813) 251-3652

DD Allen
Pierce-Allen
New York, N.Y.
(212) 627-5440

Gae Aulenti
Milan, Italy
(011 39) 025-280-2613

Tina Beebe
Moore, Ruble, Yudell
Santa Monica, Calif.
(310) 450-1400

Barry Berkus
B3 Architects/Berkus Design Studio
Santa Barbara, Calif.
(805) 966-1547

Bruce Bernbaum
Bernbaum/Magadini Architects
Dallas, Tex.
(214) 521-4531

José Solis Betancourt
Solis Betancourt
Washington, D.C.
(202) 659-8734

Jeffrey Biben
Biben + Bosley Architecture
Claremont, Calif.
(909) 624-8601

Jeffrey Bilhuber
Bilhuber, Inc.
New York, N.Y.
(212) 308-4888

Laura Bohn
LBDA
New York, N.Y.
(212) 645-3636

Laurence Booth
Booth, Hansen & Associates
Chicago, Ill.
(312) 427-0300

Peggy Bosley
Biben + Bosley Architecture
Claremont, Calif.
(909) 624-8601

Nancy Braithwaite
Nancy Braithwaite Interiors
Atlanta, Ga.
(404) 355-1740

Sheila Bridges
Sheila Bridges Design
New York, N.Y.
(212) 678-6872

Thomas Britt
Thomas Britt, Inc.
New York, N.Y.
(212) 752-9870

Mario Buatta
Mario Buatta, Inc.
New York, N.Y.
(212) 988-6811

Sue Burgess
Burgess Interiors
Chevy Chase, Md.
(301) 652-6217

Stephen Byrns
Byrns, Kendall & Schieferdecker
    Architects
New York, N.Y.
(212) 807-9600

Libby Cameron
Libby Cameron LLC
Larchmont, N.Y.
(914) 833-3885

Jane Churchill
Jane Churchill Interiors
London, England
(011 44) 1-71-730-8564

Pietro Cicognani
Cicognani Kalla
New York, N.Y.
(212) 308-4811

Celeste Cooper
Repertoire
Boston, Mass.
(617) 426-3865

Robert Couturier
Robert Couturier, Inc.
New York, N.Y.
(212) 463-7177

Joyce Crawford
Phoenix, Ariz.
(602) 952-0080

Jack DeBartolo, Jr.
DeBartolo Architects
Phoenix, Ariz.
(602) 264-6617

Roger de Cabrol
New York, N.Y.
(212) 353-2827

Maddalena De Padova
è De Padova
Milan, Italy
(011 39) 027-600-8413

Gilles Depardon
Ogawa/Depardon Architects
New York, N.Y.
(212) 627-7390

Orlando Diaz-Azcuy
Orlando Diaz-Azcuy Designs
San Francisco, Calif.
(415) 362-4500

Mary Douglas Drysdale
Drysdale, Inc.
Washington, D.C.
(202) 588-0700

Gep Durenberger
Le Sueur, Minn.
(507) 665-6855

Joe D'Urso
D'Urso Design
East Hampton, N.Y.
(516) 329-3634

David Easton
Rammed Earth Works
Napa, Calif.
(707) 224-2532

David Anthony Easton
David Anthony Easton, Inc.
New York, N.Y.
(212) 334-3820

Steven Ehrlich
Culver City, Calif.
(310) 838-9700

Merrill Elam
Scogin Elam and Bray
Atlanta, Ga.
(404) 525-6869

Beverly and Rebecca Ellsley
Beverly Ellsley Collection
Westport, Conn.
(203) 227-1157

Peter Ermacora
E.G.H Peter, Inc.
Norfolk, Conn.
(860) 542-5221

Richard Fernau
Fernau & Hartman
Berkeley, Calif.
(510) 848-4480

J. Frank Fitzgibbons
Fitzgibbons Associates Architects
Los Angeles, Calif.
(213) 663-7579

Peter Forbes
Peter Forbes and Associates Architects
Boston, Mass.
(323) 542-1760

Jonathan S. Foster
New York, N.Y.
(212) 242-7187

Tom Fox
Fox Nahem Design
New York, N.Y.
(212) 929-1485

Kenneth Garcia
Abell-Garcia Architects
Tampa, Fla.
(813) 251-3652

Mariette Himes Gomez
Gomez Associates
New York, N.Y.
(212) 288-6856

John Grable
Lake/Flato Architects
San Antonio, Tex.
(210) 227-3335

Jacques Grange
Paris, France
(011 33) 1-47-03-44-55

Michael Graves
Michael Graves, Inc.
Princeton, N.J.
(609) 924-6409

Gail Green
Green & Co.
New York, N.Y.
(212) 909-0396

Veere Grenney
Veere Grenney Associates
London, England
(011 44) 1-71-351-7170

Ronald Grimaldi
Rose Cummings
New York, N.Y.
(212) 758-0844

Carolyn Guttilla
Plaza One Interior Design
New York, N.Y.
(212) 439-6673

Victoria Hagan
Victoria Hagan Interiors
New York, N.Y.
(212) 888-1178

Robert G. Hammond
Hammond Associates
Annapolis, Md.
(410) 267-6041

Mark Hampton, Inc.
New York, N.Y.
(212) 753-4110

Stephen Harby
Santa Monica, Calif.
(310) 450-8239

Gisue and Mojgan Hariri
New York, N.Y.
(212) 727-0338

Laura Hartman
Fernau & Hartman
Berkeley, Calif.
(510) 848-4480

Nicholas Haslam
Nicholas Haslam, Inc.
London, England
(011 44) 1-71-244-8671

David Hicks
London, England
(011 44) 1-71-734-3183

William Hodgins
William Hodgins, Inc.
Boston, Mass.
(617) 262-9538

Steven and Cathi House
House + House Architects
San Francisco, Calif.
(415) 474-2112

Evan Hughes
E.G.H Peter, Inc.
Norfolk, Conn.
(860) 542-5221

Brad Huntzinger
Ironies
Berkeley, Calif.
(510) 562-9211

Hugh Newell Jacobsen
Washington, D.C.
(202) 337-5200

Greg Jordan
Greg Jordan Interior Decoration
New York, N.Y.
(212) 570-4470

Ann Kalla
Cicognani Kalla
New York, N.Y.
(212) 308-4811

Jerry Allen Kler
Jerry Allen Kler & Associates
Sausalito, Calif.
(415) 332-3868

Susan Lanier
Lubowicki/Lanier Architects
El Segundo, Calif.
(310) 322-0211

Max Levy
Max Levy Architect
Dallas, Tex.
(214) 368-2023

Christian Liaigre
Liaigre Design
Paris, France
(011 33) 1-47-53-78-76

James Light
Mallory James Interiors
Portland, Maine
(207) 773-0180

Wayne S. Lloyd
Lloyd & Tryk Associates
Santa Fe, N.Mex.
(505) 988-9789

Gary Lovejoy
Gary Lovejoy Associates
Washington, D.C.
(202) 333-5200

Paul Lubowicki
Lubowicki/Lanier Architects
El Segundo, Calif.
(310) 322-0211

Stephen Mallory
Stephen Mallory Associates
New York, N.Y.
(212) 879-9500

Gretchen Mann
Lyme, Conn.
(860) 434-2060

Mallory Marshall
Mallory James Interiors
Portland, Maine
(207) 773-0180

Melanie Martin
San Francisco, Calif.
(415) 454-8709

Kate McIntyre
Ironies
Berkeley, Calif.
(510) 644-2100

Frédéric Méchiche
Gallerie Méchiche
Paris, France
(011 33) 1-42-78-78-28

Lynn Morgan
Lynn Morgan Design
South Norwalk, Conn.
(203) 854-5037

Charles G. Mueller
Centerbrook Architects and
    Planners
Centerbrook, Conn.
(860) 767-0175

Stephen Muse
Muse-Wiedemann Architects
Washington, D.C.

Joe Nahem
Fox Nahem Design
New York, N.Y.
(212) 929-1485

Thomas O'Brien
Aero Studio
New York, N.Y.
(212) 966-4700

Kathryn Ogawa
Ogawa/Depardon Architects
New York, N.Y.
(212) 627-7390

Angèle Parlange
New Orleans, La.
(504) 897-6511

Marie-Paule Pellé
Paris, France
(011 33) 6-12-11-22-86

Dan Phipps
Dan Phipps & Associates
San Francisco, Calif.
(415) 776-1606

Carolyn Quartermaine
London, England
(011 44) 1-71-373-4491

Rob Wellington Quigley
San Diego, Calif.
(619) 232-0888

Frank Babb Randolph
Frank Babb Randolph Interior
    Design
Washington, D.C.
(202) 944-2120

Debora K. Reiser
RUR Architecture
Dobbs Ferry, N.Y.
(914) 693-0336

Michael E. Reynolds
Solar Survival Architecture
Taos, N.Mex.
(505) 751-0462

Jefferson B. Riley
Centerbrook Architects and
    Planners
Centerbrook, Conn.
(860) 767-0175

Spruce Roden
VSF
New York, N.Y.
(212) 206-7236

John Saladino
Saladino Group
New York, N.Y.
(212) 684-6805

Monique and Sergio Savarese
Dialogica
New York, N.Y.
(212) 966-1934

Tom Scheerer
Charlston, S.C.
(843) 723-0218

Daen Scheiber
Scheiber Design Group
San Francisco, Calif.
(415) 558-8833

April Sheldon
April Sheldon Design
San Francisco, Calif.
(415) 541-7773

Stephen Shubel
Stephen Shubel Studio
Sausalito, Calif.
(415) 332-8292

Charles Spada
Charles Spada Interiors
Boston, Mass.
(617) 951-0008

Michael Stanley
Putnam, Conn.
(860) 928-1419

Alexandra Stoddard
Alexandra Stoddard, Inc.
New York, N.Y.
(212) 289-5509

Jonathan Straley
Jonathan Straley Design
San Francisco, Calif.
(415) 255-1295

Emily Summers
Emily Summers Design
Dallas, Tex.
(214) 871-9669

Tom Vanderbeck
T. F. Vanderbeck Antiques
Old Lyme, Conn.
(860) 434-2349

Lynn von Kersting
Indigo Seas
Los Angeles, Calif.
(310) 550-8758

Troy P. Walker
Troy P. Walker Design Services
San Francisco, Calif.
(415) 431-3077

Alan Wanzenberg
Johnson & Wanzenberg
New York, N.Y.
(212) 489-7840

Lisa Weiss
The Weiss Company
Tiburon, Calif.
(415) 435-8182

Toby West
Toby West Limited
Atlanta, Ga.
(404) 233-7425

Samuel G. White
Buttrick White & Burtis
New York, N.Y.
(212) 967-3333

John F. Wilson IV
Manteo on Roanoke Island, N.C.
(919) 473-3282

Vicente Wolf
Vicente Wolf & Associates
New York, N.Y.
(212) 465-0590

Buzz Yudell
Moore, Ruble, Yudell
Santa Monica, Calif.
(310) 450-1400

PHOTOGRAPHY CREDITS

1: Lisl Dennis

2–4: Jeff McNamara

6: Judith Watts

8: Oberto Gili

10: William Waldron

12: Fernando Bengoechea

14: Antoine Bootz

16: Laura Resen

18: Peter Margonelli

19: Scott Frances

20: Jeff Goldberg/Esto

21: Scott Frances

22–23: Jeff McNamara

24: Jeremy Samuelson

25: Richard Felber

26: Kari Haavisto

27: Thibault Jeanson

28: Scott Frances

30–31: Thibault Jeanson

32: Tim Street-Porter

33: Christopher Irion

34–35: Antoine Bootz

36–37: Jeremy Samuelson

38: Timothy Hursley

40: Dominique Vorillon

42: Tim Street-Porter

43: Timothy Hursley

44: Peter Aaron

45: Timothy Hursley

46–47: Jack Winston

48–49: Tim Street-Porter

50: Gordon Beall

51: Christopher Irion

52: William Waldron

53: Jeff McNamara (top)

53: William Waldron (bottom)

54: John Vaughan

55: Jacques Dirand

56: Tim Street-Porter

57: Judith Watts

58–59: Robert Lautman

60: Scott Frances

61: Christopher Irion

62: J. D. Peterson

63: Walter Smalling

64: Judith Watts

65: Dominique Vorillon

66: Laura Resen

67: Thibault Jeanson

68: Jesse Gerstein

69: Fernando Bengoechea

70: Victoria Pearson

71: Laura Resen

72: Thibault Jeanson

73: Mark Darley

74: Christopher Irion

76: Dominique Vorillon

77: John Sutton

78: Oberto Gili

79: John Hall

80–81: Langdon Clay

82: William Waldron

83–84: Timothy Hursley

85: Christopher Irion

86: Oberto Gili

88: Tim Street-Porter

90–93: Oberto Gili

94: Anne Gummerson

95: Andrew Lawson

96: Alex McClean (top)

96: Antoine Bootz (bottom)

97: Thibault Jeanson

98: Fernando Bengoechea

99–101: Antoine Bootz

102: Scott Frances

103: Antoine Bootz

104: Alexandre Bailhache

105–107: Elizabeth Zeschin

108: Peter Margonelli

109–111: Thibault Jeanson

112: Walter Smalling

113: Lisl Dennis

114: Antoine Bootz

116: Langdon Clay

117: John Vaughan

118: Kari Haavisto

119: Robert Lautman

120: Antoine Bootz

121: Lizzie Himmel

122: Michael Dunne

123: Robert Starkoff (left)

123: Scott Frances (right)

124: Peter Vitale

125: Paul Whicheloe

126: Richard Felber

127: Christopher Simon Sykes

128: Kari Haavisto

129: Antoine Bootz

130: Scott Frances

131: Thibault Jeanson

132: Scott Frances

134: Jeff McNamara

135: Michael Mundy

136: Michael Dunne

137: Jack Winston

138: Scott Frances (top)

138: Antoine Bootz (bottom)

139: Thibault Jeanson

140: Tim Street-Porter

141: James Mortimer

142: Steve Tague

144: Michael Mundy

145–146: Jacques Dirand

147: Antoine Bootz

148: Thibault Jeanson (left)

148: Antoine Bootz (right)

149: Gordon Beall

150: Christopher Simon Sykes (top)

150: Paul Whicheloe (bottom)

151: Gordon Beall

152: Laura Resen

153: Peter Margonelli

154: Alexandre Bailhache (left)

154: Steve Tague (right)

155: Jacques Dirand

156: Billy Cunningham (top)

156: Gordon Beall (bottom)

157: Richard Felber

158: Lizzie Himmel

159: Gordon Beall

160: Jeff McNamara

162: Richard Felber

163: Andrew Garn

164: Karen Radkai

165: Antoine Bootz

167: William Waldron

168: John Coolidge

171: Jacques Dirand

172: Dominique Vorillon

174: Alex McClean

176: William Waldron

The room on page 1 was designed by Wayne Lloyd and Joyce Crawford; page 2, Pietro Cicognani, Ann Kalla, Laura Bohn, and Joseph Lembo; page 4, Vicente Wolf; page 6, Michael Graves; page 8, Eero Saarinen; page 10, Victoria Hagan; page 12, Roger de Cabrol; page 14, Maddalena De Padova; page 167, Nancy Braithwaite; page 168, Lynn Morgan; page 171, David Hicks; page 172, Stephen Shubel; page 174, Tom Fox and Joe Nahem; page 176, Mallory Marshall and James Light; front jacket, Kate McIntyre and Brad Huntzinger; back jacket, Pietro Cicognani, Ann Kalla, Laura Bohn, and Joseph Lembo.